SIBERIA

by

Israel Emiot

Translated by Leah Zazuyer

with

Brina Menachovsky Rose

State Street Press Chapbooks, 1991

ACKNOWLEDGEMENTS:

"My God I Believe in You So Much . . . ," "A Prayer in Nineteen Forty-Three," "Prayer of a Man in Snow," and "With or Without Me . . ." were published in these translations in *The Seneca Review*, Vol. XXI, No. 1, Spring 1991.

"My God I Believe in You So Much . . ," translated by Stanley Kunitz, appeared in *A Treasury of Yiddish Poetry*, edited by Irving Howe and Eliezer Greenberg, Holt, Rhinehart, Winston, NY, 1969.

This chapbook is made possible with support from the Literature Program of the New York State Council on the Arts.

Cover illustration: Harry A. Siegerman, from an original woodcut in *Jewish Folk Dances*, Nathan Vizonsky, American-Hebrew Theatrical League, Chicago, 1942.

Back Cover Illustration: Aaron Braveman, from an original lino-cut, "These are the Names"--The Book of Exodus, 1974.

Yiddish typography--Gitl Schaechter-Viswanath, Teaneck, NJ and also Saul Berman, Toronto, Canada

Printed at Monroe Reprographics

Editor: Judith Kitchen

State Street Press
P.O. Box 278
Brockport, NY 14420

Dedicated to Libbe Berman, my first Yiddish teacher, and a contributor to this book in manifold ways

INTRODUCTION

Only one thing remained reachable, close and secure
amid all losses: language . . ."

— Paul Celan, Bremen Prize Award, Germany

Israel Emiot probably wrote parts of four of the poems in this collection on cigarette papers while he was a political prisoner in eastern Siberia from 1948 to 1956. Some others he simply committed to memory. Since pen was forbidden, writing was a punishable act during the seven years Emiot spent in a variety of hard labor camps near the city of Taishet, some 3000 miles from Moscow.

In many ways, Emiot was the classic twentieth-century Jewish refugee. He was born in 1909 in Ostrov-Mazowiecka, northwest of Warsaw. One quarter of its forty thousand inhabitants were Jews. After an impoverished childhood within Poland's rich Hasidic tradition and its educational strictures, he provided himself with a secular education. Although he attended various yeshivas and was slated to become a rabbi, Emiot furtively read the books his father had left behind when he went to America in 1919, hoping to become a doctor, but dying a presser in New York City in 1922.

When Emiot was fifteen, his mother and grandmother became concerned that he spent so much time on poetry. Thus they arranged that he would go to Lublin to prepare for the rabbinate. In 1926, at the age of seventeen, they arranged his marriage in the Hasidic tradition. However, this did not curtail his literary activities. For example, he met and was influenced by Israel Shtern.

By 1926 he was writing for various orthodox publications such as the *Bes Jacov Journal* and *Dos Yiddishe Togblatt*, and had had a poem published in Hebrew in *Our Hope*, an important anthology edited by I. M. Weissenberg. Emiot soon also became involved with the Warsaw Literary Circle and "Tlomatka," The House of the Jewish Writers Union. Eventually his early religious supporters and publishers began to question his piety, his evolving content, his use of a pseudonym possibly based on his father's secularized name, and the switch from Hebrew to Yiddish as his writing language. His poems began appearing in the Yiddish language journal *Zu Kunft*, etc Between 1932 and 1938, Emiot published four books of poems.

As the German army invaded Poland in 1939, Emiot fled not to Vilnius in Lithuania, the historic center of Jewish intellectual orthodoxy, but to Bialystok in the nearby Soviet Union. Ironically, for this understandable act, he was judged harshly by some who survived the infamous Warsaw Ghetto. Meanwhile his mother, who had insisted on remaining in their hometown, was killed by the Germans and buried in a mass grave. Throughout his life, Emiot took emotional refuge from this trauma in his writings.

When the German army advanced into Russia, the Soviet government sent many refugees east by train, to join work batallions. Emiot's wife and children arrived in the vicinity of Alma Ata, in Kazakhstan, where they remained in dire conditions until 1945 when they began making their way west, eventually settling in Rochester, NY in the early 1950s.

Emiot's life during these years was more complicated. "Prayer in 1943" documents his presence in Alma Ata, but it is not known how long and under what circumstances he was there. He spent some of the war years in Moscow, where he became part of the Moscow Jewish Literary Circle which then included the famous writers Der Nister and Bergelson, as well as Markish and others from his Warsaw days. By his own account, his time in Moscow was happy both personally and artistically. Indeed, a chapbook of his poems, titled *Lider*, was published by the official Russian-Jewish printing house Der Emes (The Truth) in 1940, and contained a laudatory introduction by an approved Soviet critic.

Whether it was first in Moscow or Alma Ata, Emiot wrote articles on the wartime plight and life of Jewish refugees in the Soviet Far East, and these came to the attention of the Soviet-sponsored Joint Anti-Fascist Committee. In 1944, Emiot was invited to move to Birobidzhan (the first Autonomous Jewish Soviet-Socialist Republic) as a journalist for the Committee. Thus Emiot began, as both a journalist and a creative writer, to document and extol the dream-become-reality of a Soviet Jewish homeland. However, he was not unaware, even then, of the controversy among Jews over the hazards of supporting the establishment and the concept of Birobidzhan. After all, the Soviets had alternately sanctioned and repressed Jewish life throughout the thirties and early forties.

While Emiot had become actively involved in the revitalization of Jewish culture in the Soviet Union, the concept itself met with a variety of political responses. It soon became apparent that the political winds were shifting again. Stalin and his associates began to censor, persecute, imprison, and even murder numbers of leading Jewish artists, intellectuals, and professionals throughout the country. Thus it was that Emiot--a refugee from Hasidic Judaism, whose work had artistically and joyously incorporated some homage to socialism since 1940, and whose 1947 book, *Rising,* printed in Birobidzhan, was heavy with obligatory socialist canon-- was nevertheless tried in absentia in Moscow, and sentenced to ten years of hard labor. He was accused of advocating Jewish culture, and of various other crimes of Jewish "internationalism."

After the Khrushchev-era commutation of part of his sentence (which, ironically, he had already served), and his eventual release, Emiot, although physically and spiritually diminished, made his way back to Birobidzhan where his amnestized but not "rehabilitated" status rendered life extremely problematic. In 1957, he returned to Poland where he was eligible for some recuperative time in a sanitorium. Interviewed there by journalist S. L. Schneiderman, Emiot still dared speak only in furtive whispers. Nevertheless, he was able to produce a quantity of poetry and other writings. Thus, by 1957, soon after his return to his native Poland, two of the present cycle of twenty-two poems he called "Siberia" had already been published in Yiddish in a book titled *Yearning*.

In 1958, Emiot made his way to New York. Shortly after his arrival in the United States, Emiot accepted an invitation for a three-month sponsored "historical tour" of Israel. The trip was a great success and bolstered his spirits. He was invited to return and become a member of a writers' kibbutz. In 1959, he made application for permanent immigration status to Israel. However, it is said that the night before his departure he suffered a heart attack, and was thus once again thwarted in obtaining the refuge he sought.

It is unclear just when and how he was reunited with his, by now, estranged family in Rochester, NY. He settled there, struggling to make money, regain his health, and establish a literary life in yet a new language. During his last fifteen years, he became Writer-in-Residence for the Jewish Community Center and edited a tri-lingual literary journal called *Roots*. He continued to write, publish, and lecture until his death, in Rochester, in 1978.

Ironically, even in his years in the United States, ideological issues still haunted him. There were still those who condemned his slackening orthodoxy. At the same time, there were those who accused him of being a communist and/or of having a misguided investment in Birobidzhan. When Emiot's ship docked in New York harbor in 1958, a representative from a Yiddish newspaper came to meet him. Because a Yiddish newspaper in Buenos Aires had printed the "fact" that Emiot was a KGB agent, the journalist feared that Emiot was in danger. In addition Emiot, no longer a Hosed or even very observant, was often cast, by virtue of his knowledge, background, and heritage, into the role of the illusive "Tsadek," or spiritual guru. Thus Emiot had to deal with the full brunt of the post-Khrushchev disarray and realignment of the American Jewish community. This was true in every city where he visited or lectured. It was particularly vivid in his fairly extensive contacts with the Jewish literary community in New York City

In fact, Emiot was essentially apolitical, only moderately affiliated with religious institutions, and more interested in profane than in sacred love. Emiot's own words sum up his dilemma: "A writer, an artist, is always alone." It was through the literary friendships he made in Rochester, his enjoyment of music, and his writing that Emiot found the wherewithal to maintain his core identity, for, as Chaim Grade, distinguished Yiddish poet and novelist, wrote in a letter to him in 1957, "We don't even have a minyan by now in Yiddish literature."

Emiot wrote two very different versions of his incarceration. In a prose memoir (misleadingly titled *The Birobidzhan Affair*, translated by Max Rosenfeld and published in 1981 by the Jewish Publication Society of

America), Emiot began by detailing his year in a local jail awaiting judgment and sentence. Thrown in with vicious and petty common criminals, and often in isolation, he was constantly interrogated, ill-fed, and ill-exercised. He considered suicide, but survived in part because of his surprise at his ability to cope and his initiation into the wall finger-tapping code used by the prisoners as a means of communication.

There followed transportation (a long, difficult Soviet-style journey by train) to the labor camps in Siberia. Despite a variety of different locales, levels of labor, camp conditions, health crises, severe climate, and, in addition, anti-semitism and anti-intellectualism on the part of both prisoners and officials, Emiot endured his seven years. How? Certainly with luck. Also with a writer's curiosity, some cunning, and the company of other wonderful and courageous prisoners. There is much evidence that Emiot himself provided emotional support and critical physical assistance to others as well.

The prose memoir is a gripping and sober saga of a man whose life had been almost exclusively of the mind, whose body and soul learned a different kind of rigor. It is reportage and story-telling. Many have already noted its striking absence of bitterness, self-pity, or undue emotionality and its vivid and astute description of other people. The prose memoir was written to tell the world about the Gulag.

The second version is found in this sequence of poems, collected under the title of "Siberia." By 1961, twenty-one of the "Siberia" poems were included, with numerous others, in a book called *In Melody Absorbed*, printed in Yiddish in Rochester, NY, by its Jewish Community Federation. A prologue poem was added when they were reprinted in the 1966 Yiddish language collection, *Before You Extinguish Me*, published privately. That poem was actually composed in 1943, but apparently Emiot felt that the wartime suffering which suffuses the poem was an appropriate beginning for his Siberian cycle.

Only in "Siberia" does Emiot reveal his despair, his effort to sustain contact with reality, his intense internal dialogues, the refuge he took in memories of his traditional and protective childhood, his guilt over having abandoned his early religiosity, the interminability of the experience, his bargainings with God, his prison relationships, and, yes, his anger. Only the poems finally reveal to us what we really need to know--how and with what terrors and graces a human being must survive his fate. In the poems we see, too, that memory was clearly Emiot's lifelong refuge.

The twenty-two Siberia poems are complex in both form and content. Nevertheless, they have a striking organicity, which flows from their carefully crafted sequencing of mood, event, and tone. The poems divide into three types: twelve are flawless Petrarchan sonnets, rhymed in the original Yiddish. Another seven are addresses to God, a particularly flexible and distinctly Jewish genre, though not exclusively so. (Rilke, among others, used this device.) These poems have a looser, longer line, with or without rhyme and stanza breaks. Finally, three briefer poems and one longer one are more personal and in free verse.

It is no accident that Emiot begins the cycle with twelve sonnets: that form lends itself well to meditation, problem-solving, or questioning in poetry. Nor is it accidental that Emiot chose the Petrarchan form of the sonnet which pivots after eight lines, rather than the Shakespearian form which pivots more tidily in the last couplet.

The reader will notice the subtitle "Dreamsongs" preceding the first sonnet. Emiot did not indicate where the Dreamsongs end. If they are the first eleven, then what about the fourteenth? Or are they simply all the sonnets? Perhaps the ambiguity was intended, for the Dreamsongs clearly convey Emiot's psychic vacillation between the day and night dreams of his early life in Poland and his prison reality. Yet in both content and structure they gradually shift the focus of the poems from retreat to confrontation. Emiot (like the poet John Berryman who also used this title) was clearly aware of the archetypal significance of the dream state.

Each Dreamsong begins with an octet memory of some intense and pleasant aspect of his securely traditional childhood surrounded by significant elders. The poem then pivots on his use of this memory as a platform from which to dive into the six lines which confront reality. Moreover, the relationship between the two grows complex: sometimes the memory helps make sense of the reality; sometimes the memory is so real it makes the actual reality seem questionably surreal, and even distant or emotionally remote.

With the first sonnet, Emiot sets up an equivalence between time and distance: "...as much distance from me to me/ as from Poland to Siberia." By the fifth and sixth, the dream gives way to reality. The eighth sonnet, with its esoteric and metaphysical Kabbalistic beliefs, tries to make sense of the horror. Its sestet is interrrupted by a curious dotted line. Some poets, including Rilke, have used this device variously. For Emiot it appears to express a sharp break and/or a heightening of his emotional tone. The ninth sonnet actually begins in Siberia and stresses reality. In the tenth and eleventh sonnets, which also begin in the camp, Emiot tries on the extremes of selfless piety and ironic humor, but cannot succeed totally at either. Thus the fourteenth, and last, sonnet is strikingly secular, referring not only to the Polish composer Oginski, but obliquely to a loving "you."

Gradually, over the course of these Dreamsongs, a remarkable evolution ensues, in which the present experience moves into the octet and his past moves into the body of the sestet, i.e. they reverse themselves within the form and in their relationship to reality and memory. Denial and grief become less essential to the voice of the poems. His use of the prayer-to-God cannot be fully utilized until that basic transition has occurred, for the prayers acknowledge the reality of his incarceration.

The sonnets contain another progression. Emiot recalls Pesach, Sukes, Shabes, Rosheshone, Yon Kiper and Shavues in that order. The very fact that the holidays appear in a non-sequential order indicates his personalization of the material and heightens the quality of childhood memory. The sonnets also divide between the topics of workdays and holidays, whereby work is reality and holidays symbolize memories and are dream-like. In another striking switch, Emiot's sonnets are in some important respects more pious in tone than his prayers.

The Siberian cycle ends with some weariness and despair over the human condition and the futility of much that has occurred. Emiot does not believe that suffering is redemptive. Yet it is mediated by the celebration of the ordinary and daily, the effort to leave something for the next generation, and the denial of human death as unique in the natural cycle of life and death.

An astonishing number of great poets in an equally astonishing array of countries have been political prisoners in the last century. Among such poets, the works of Anna Akhmatova, Osip Mandelstam, and Vladimir Mayakovsky were known to Emiot. These Russian poets exemplify a variety of responses to the prison experience. Mayakovsky vacillated between lyricism, socialist content, and linguistic play, breaking his usual quatrain into columns. Though he appeared to be a *bon vivant* while incarcerated, he later committed suicide. Mandelstam's response was also a drastic shift to a less formal, more satiric and symbolist poetry. However, his writing diminished in prison and he died insane, lamenting, "I have forgotten the word." Akhmatova's response to her imprisonment and the execution of her ex-husband can be read in her shifts between a calm and an agitated voice, using both the first and second person. She obsessively recorded every possible detail and face from her prison life, believing that sin and frivolity were to blame for her misfortune.

Similarly, Emiot's concern is not his innocence but his guilt. In many of the poems there is an undertext that asks if straying from strict traditions has visited this suffering upon him. Is he being punished not so much by the Soviets as by God? Therefore, in some poems, he bargains with God. Emiot's thrust is reminiscent of Job's, but less angry or overt. Certainly his anger is not directed at the political process of which he is a victim, although the special hardship of being a Jewish political prisoner fuels his introspection. By contrast with the Russians, Emiot's incarceration led to a more formal poetics.

However diverse it is, all prison literature is constrained by some basic issues: the meaning of the experience, whether suffering can be seen as redemptive, the purpose of the act of writing itself. Typically a grief process ensues. Perhaps the incarcerated poet's use of nature and memory are most vividly illustrated in the work of Abraham Sutzkever, the legendary writer and editor who survived the Vilna ghetto and now lives in Israel. Nature has order. Furthermore, it lives in memory; it is beyond obliteration. Thus the act of poetry-making itself is experienced as having regenerative powers--personally and for humanity--just as much or more than the traditional Jewish emphasis on *a priori* study and knowledge. Unlike Sutzkever, Emiot never explicitly states his belief that he will survive if he writes, but it is certainly implicit.

In the end, Emiot steered a fairly middle course between objectivity and subjectivity when prison writing in general is considered. In fact, the lack of political content in Emiot's poetry is striking. It stands in direct contrast to the work of such writers as Faiz Ahmed Faiz, Nazim Hikmet, Yannis Ritsos, Vaclav Havel, Nelson Mandela, Wole Soyinka, Cesare Pavese, Cesar Vallejo and Pablo Neruda. Emiot never even conceived of doing for either Poland or Jewish Poland what Neruda did for Chile. His response more closely resembled that of the Polish poet Zbigniew Herbert, who wrote from an occupied Poland that "we are despite everything/ the guardians of our brothers." Thus we see that incarceration often creates a strongly generalized and heightened concern for all of humanity.

In addition to his imprisonment, another profound influence on Emiot's poetry is the long tradition of Yiddish literature. Its roots go back to bardic and minstrel times. In Uriel Weinreich's discussion of Yiddish poetry and its infusion, he refers to its early influence and stylization via medieval Germanic poetic traditions, the Bible, Hebrew liturgical tradition, melody and chant, and its employment of Italianate ottava rima rhyme schemes. During the nineteenth century, it owed much of its forms to folksong and Hasidic tale.

Scholars Uriel Weinreich, Irving Howe, Ruth R. Wisse, Khone Shmuruk, Benjamin and Barbara Harshav, and Aaron Kramer see emigration and urbanization as the first modernizers of Yiddish poetry. In America, a generation of "sweat-shop" poets recast the traditional ballad and folksong into a political and highly socially conscious genre. But the ultimate modernization of Yiddish poetry was heralded by a group of writers called "Di Yunge" (The Young). Formed in the U. S. in the early part of this century, they were led by the poet Yehoash. Other groups were formed simultaneously in Canada, Russia, and Poland. Di Yunge's 1907 Manifesto asserted an individual, non-political diction, voice, and content. "No longer do we wish to be the rhyme department of the Jewish Labor movement," wrote Landau.

The full flowering came with a group called In Zich (In Self) or the "introspectivists." Their 1919 Manifesto demonstrated the Yiddish poet's awareness of and allegiance to a totally personalized form and content which drew heavily on European expressionism and other modernist movements, and rejected the notion of a necessary dichotomy between the heart and mind of the poet. They saw form and content as one, and insisted the poet's first responsibility was to his inner voice. According to scholar Itche Goldberg, whereas in the nineteenth century's literature self-blame or despair predictably follows weakening of faith or social conscience, in the later humanistic tradition, exemplified by Peretz, man himself becomes central.

The Di Yunge poets were not unorthodox prosodists; however, they were concerned with musicality and sensuality. Irving Howe points out that, lacking a classical tradition, Yiddish poetry had to embody the best classical elements simultaneously with a movement toward romanticism. But the In Zich component of the modernist movement was a profound break with the past since there had originally been no tradition of secular imaginative art.

Scholar Dan Miron postulates yet another break: the experimental nature of Yiddish poetry was followed by a return to poetic conservatism after the war and the Holocaust. However, Emiot does not fit neatly into these broad trends because the Siberia poems revert to traditional forms in combination with the use of modern elements. In fact, Emiot's most lyric, pastoral, and nostalgic poetry follows his orthodox period, survives his transplant into Russia, continues up to his time in Birobidzhan, and flowers in the United States.

Goldberg has written that Yiddish literature has an embivalence, a tension between faith and scepticism, despair and hope, laughter and tears. One persistent theme in Yiddish poetry is the quarrel with God. Yiddish poets carry on a most intimate and egalitarian dialogue with God in which he can be chastized, scolded, reminded, thanked, treated with childlike humility or lavish hope and expectation. It is never a dialogue initiated by a sinner or directed at a wrathful potentate. Thus, in the Prologue poem, Emiot struggles with an inability to praise God; he therefore praises nature, which he not only sees as God's handiwork, but which he uses to remind God of his power for goodness. By the twelfth poem, he bargains, acknowledging the duality of good and evil. He turns God's commandment back on Him, asking that God do unto him as man is supposed to do unto God. The fifteenth poem questions God; it is a prayer in praise of the thinking man. The sixteenth protests that God has abandoned man and the seventeenth prays that God will intercede between man and the wrongs of the world.

The reader will note a progression in these prayer poems--they grow increasingly bolder. This tone is reflected in the form. They move from four or five structured quatrains to freer verse, and finally use the model of a famous secular Polish poem by Slowacki. The use of a secular model has its own message in terms of a statement about faith. However, the last prayer poem returns to a measured quatrain as Emiot again empowers his God.

Emiot sometimes uses the classic Biblical syntactic of parallelism and restatement. For example, he says "and look, behold." Or he writes "perhaps/ is it possible," using first a lofty Hebrew Bible-invoking phrase which has infused Yiddish, and then a restatement in more intimate Yiddish words. This use of the poetic doublet was also common in the split between traditional church and everyday Slavonic languages, but is more subtle than our modern-day use of slang.

Emiot taught himself several languages in the course of his life but he had, at the very least, read Whitman, Emerson, Byron, Keats, Shelley,

Shakespeare, Tagore, Bialik, and many Russians in Yiddish translation. However, Rainer Maria Rilke (whose work he may have read in its original German) was Emiot's life-long literary soul mate and, to some extent, his model. Emiot responded to Rilke's psychological homelessness. In his meditative poems, Rilke engages in a reflective process; Emiot's poems are more lament. Rilke wrote, "You must change your life." Emiot cries that he has *had* to change his!

Rilke's influence is most strongly felt in the poems that address God. Rilke's *Book of Hours* is full of addresses to God, with whom he sought a mystical union. The most striking aspect of these poems is his empathy with God, which of course implies identity: "What will you do when I die God . . . I am afraid . . ." implying that God will die as and when man dies. By contrast, Emiot's most natural mode of address to God is dominated by expressions of hardship and complaint, alternating with an acknowledgement of His power. He does not seek union but rapport-- along with a decent, if separate, identity for man: "My God, don't put to shame your very own human being, your jewels!" In both cases, the person addressing God is identified with the role of the Artist, or Creator.

One other influence on Emiot's Siberian sequence is music. In the final sonnet, he refers to the Polish composer Oginski's *Polonaise*. Oginski becomes a symbol for Emiot's specific longing for a long-dead or dying way of life. Music sustains Emiot in this poem because it symbolizes the metaphysical problem of where music, and all else, resides when it leaves us and enters memory. Music also proves to Emiot that he is still alive, just as music in the labor camp united diverse Jews, who found or made instruments and played together when possible. In the fourth sonnet, Emiot alludes to the playing of the Kol Nidre by a talented but fatally-ill prisoner; the sound mesmerizes and unites them so that they are able to defy the authorities one more time.

In one poem, the refrain of a popular Yiddish folksong about rain sets the tone. In "Prayer of a Man in Snow," an Hasidic dudele dictates the structure of the poem and its diction, and would have provided a ready symbolic frame of reference for most readers. In fact, this poem is the most symbolic in the cycle. Using an elliptical sentence structure but also a musical structure, snow simultaneously symbolizes purity, peace, emptiness, godliness, safety, and psychic numbness.

Israel Emiot died in Rochester in 1978. It is only fitting that the present chapbook, a first bilingual edition of the complete "Siberia" poems, is being published here--the final resting place in his peripatetic literary life. However, this cycle of poems is by no means his only literary output. During a writing life begun at fifteen, Emiot produced hundreds of poems, a quantity of short stories, feuilletons, a prose memoir, a significant body of essays, literary criticism, and some translations. Some of his work has been lost; much of the existing work remains untranslated. Thus the Siberian cycle represents only a small percentage of the poems which we are now in the final stages of translating. We have taken the liberty of appending two additional poems to the twenty-two original Siberia poems. The first, marked by Emiot as written in Siberia while imprisoned, is called "My Town." It is a bitter-sweet poem. The second, called "Before Spring," is a poem very dear to Emiot and reworked through the years, from 1940 to 1976. It can be taken as his theme poem in which, despite all that has happened to him, he can write, "willingly, perhaps unwillingly,/ despite my alienated and remote heart/ within me young April hums like a dove."

Note: It is customary for the translator to speak of the task. The late Yiddish poet and editor, Menke Katz, was especially insightful in contrasting the Yiddish use of a dactyl or anapest stress pattern as opposed to the typical iambic stress of English. Irving Howe refers to the Yiddish language's more generous criteria for endearment--especially via its aggregated diminutives. The availability of reflexive verbs in Yiddish adds possibilities for poignancy and self-reflection. Emiot coins new word constructions, evokes earthiness with the use of Slavonic "z" and "c" words, and uses the neutralized vowels of Yiddish to evoke a conversational tone.; these devices are all consistent with Uriel Weinreich's discussion of Yiddish poetry. Yiddish has no capitalization; therefore the use of "and" to begin a line of poetry is pertinent. While rhyme and even meter have been compromised, hopefully the sense of the poems, their stanzaic structure, Emiot's imagery and musicality, have been done justice. The reader should know that sound value is a constant in the Yiddish of Israel Emiot, whether via rhyme, assonance, or onomotopoetic devices.

Every effort has been made to avoid "elevation" of either Yiddish or English. Much has been written about the hazards of translation, but it was Isaac Bashevis Singer who said, "Yiddish is the wise and humble language of us all, the idiom of frightened and hopeful humanity."

A joyful collaboration with my Canadian co-translator, Yiddishist Brina Menachovsky Rose, has made this book possible. The translations have also been enhanced by the scrutiny of Yiddishist Elinor Robinson, Rochester Rabbis, Abraham Karp, Judea Miller, and Nechimiah Vogel are thanked for their diverse assistance. Canadian cultural leader and Yiddishist Aaron Fainer was an invaluable resource, as was Canadian educator and editor, Joseph Kligman.

For generosity with time and memories, I am deeply indebted to the former editor of *The Forwards*, Simon Weber, journalists Joshua Friedensohn and S. L. Schneiderman, author Isaac Bashevis Singer, attorney Bernard Schuster, poet Francesca Guli, cultural artists Herbert and Alice Sufrin, educator Aaron Braveman, community leaders Irving and Eugenia Ruderman, Louis and Doris Rosenstein, Manual Hoffman, Dr. Soffer, and Emiot's fellow prisoner Michael Feldman. I thank Canadian Vera Semec, widow of Ukranian patriot Dr. Miron Semec, who befriended Emiot in a camp hospital, for her generous and poignant comments. Poet Pat Janus' literary friendship with Emiot served as inspiration. While all of Emiot's poetry resides in the public domain, his family's cooperation with the translation process, in its earliest stages, is gratefully acknowledged.

Numerous Yiddish writers have contributed essential insights into Emiot's life and letters: Joseph Kerler, Sol Liptzin, and Khaim Maltinsky of Israel, Peretz Miransky and M. M. Shaffir of Canada, Lazar Ran, Gabriel Preil, and A. M. Orzicyer of New York City, and also scholar Dan Miron of Israel and New York. Reference librarian Dina Abramowicz and head librarian Zachary M. Baker, both at YIVO, made their archives and expertise available in a timely and generous manner.

Distinguished Yiddish translator and educator Max Rosenfeld, of Philadelphia, who rendered Emiot's prose memoir, has offered friendship and encouragement throughout this project, as have poets Cornelius Eady, Jim LaVilla-Havelin, Ann Githler, Shreela Ray, and Etta Ruth Weigl. We thank Herbert Rose and James, Elisa, and Ian Watson for their advice and interest.

Leah Zazuyer
Rochester, NY, 1991

On the translators:

Leah Zazuyer grew up in a Yiddish-speaking household and has studied Yiddish as an adult, both privately and at summer programs at Oxford and Columbia. Her poetry and other writings have been published in numerous literary magazines. A chapbook of her poetry is due out from FootHills Publishing in 1991. She first met Israel Emiot in literary circles in Rochester, NY, but did not start to translate his poetry until after his death.

Brina Menachovsky Rose is a Canadian who was born in Poland. Her parents were both well-known teachers of Yiddish and she is herself a Yiddishist, a teacher, and cultural worker.

סיביר

פֿון

ישראל עמיאָט

פֿאַרטײַטשט פֿון לאה זאזשוייער

און

ברײַנדל מענאַכאָווסקי ראָז

SIBERIA

by

Israel Emiot

Translated by Leah Zazuyer

with

Brina Menachovsky Rose

אַ תּפֿילה נײַנצן דרײַ און פֿערציק

ה. לאַנגן

גוטער גאָט, זע, איך בין אָרעם און פֿאַל איבער זיך אַלײַן,
און מײַן קינד טראָגט זיך דרײַ מאָל זײַן מאָס
און שפילט מיט קינדער זיך און פֿאַלט און לויפֿט צו מיר מיט געוויין
ווי איך צו דיר מיט אַ פֿאַרוואָס און אַן אַ פֿאַרוואָס.

איך ווײַס, אַז אין אַלע תּפֿילות טוט מען אַן דיך קרוינען פֿון גאָלד
און ווערטער צו דיר זײַנען די שענסטע פֿון אַלע ווערטער,
דאָך באַלײַדיק נישט די תּפֿילה פֿון אַ קינד וואָס אַלץ וואָס עס וואָלט געוואָלט
איז אַן אײגן געלעגער און מוז שלאָפֿן אויף דער ערד דער פֿערטער.

דײַן טאָג – דײַן ליד – לייען איך יעדן טאָג און באַוווּנדער,
באַוווּנדער נאָך אַלץ די לעצטע סטראָף – דײַן שקיעה,
נאָר ווען איך וויל נעמען לויבן דיך, פֿאַלן די העסט מיך אַרונטער.
אַ, שטראָף מיך נישט, דאָס העמד אויף מיר איז פֿרעמד און אויסגעליִען.

מײַן קלוגסשאַפֿט ווייסט שוין אַז דער מענטש איז קליין,
אַז די ערד איז דאָס קלענסטע פֿון אַלע דײַנע ערטער,
דאָך שטראָף מיך נישט און הער אויס דאָס געוויין
פֿון אַ קינד וואָס שלאָפֿט אויף דער ערד דער פֿערטער.

(קאַזאַכסטאַן, מלחמה־יאָרן)

A PRAYER IN NINETEEN FORTY-THREE

For H. Lang

Good God, look I'm poor, and trip over myself,
and my child wears shoes three times his size,
plays with children, falls, and runs crying to me,
as I to you — with and without a reason.

I know, all prayers crown you in gold,
and address the most exquisite words to you;
still, don't insult the prayer of a child, who just wants
his own bed, and has to sleep fourth on the ground.

Your song — the day — I read and admire daily;
I still marvel at your last verse — the sunset,
but when I want to praise you my hands fail me!
Oh do not punish me, even my shirt is borrowed.

Wisdom tells me man is insignificant,
and earth the least of all your spheres;
still, do not punish me; listen to the lament
of a child who sleeps fourth on the ground.

[Kazakhstan, war years]

חלומות

מײַן חלום גראָבט אַלץ טיף די שיכטן
פֿון מײַן קינדהײַט, פּלאַסט נאָך פּלאַסט,
אַרײַן־אַרויס גײט גאַסט נאָך גאַסט
אין אונדזער הויז, אומגעריכט איז.

און געפֿאַרבט פֿון טאָג דאָס ליכט איז,
װי מער געבראָקט מיט ניס, װי ס'פֿאַסט
פֿאַר חול־המועד, װען אונדזער גאַס
מיט אַזאַ אָװנטליכט געדיכט איז.

עלנט צי איך פֿרי די דעק אָפּ
פֿון מײַן געלעגער, פֿרײריק קאַלט
קוקט אין שויב אַרײַן דער װאַלד.

איז אַזוי פֿיל טעג און װעג אָפּ?
אַזוי פֿיל װעג פֿון מיר צו מיר
װי פֿון פּױלן קײן סיביר.

20

DREAMSONGS

My dream digs deep into the strata
of childhood, layer after layer:
in and out of our house go
guest after guest; everyone an unexpected player.

And the clear light of dawn is colored
by the day, when, like Khalemoyed mead
sprinkled with nuts,
our street is thick with such evening light.

Forlorn, I pull back the covers in early morning;
from where I've lain the freezing cold forest
looks through my window pane.

How many days and ways have passed —
as much distance from me to me
as from Poland to Siberia?

דײַן ספֿרים־שראַנק, אַ, זיידע מײַנער אָרעם,
פֿון סוכּות נאָך געבליבן אין דער שראַנק
אַן אתרוג, אויסגעטריקנט לאַנג
און שמעקט נאָך אַלץ, און סע שמעקן אַלע ספֿרים.

די זון שענקט אַ קעסטל שײַן אין דרום
און אויפֿן טיש איז אָפֿן נאָך דער דף
וואָס כ'האָב געלאָזן אין חכמה טיף פֿאַרגאַפֿט –
געוועזן אַ מענטש און איז געוואָרן וואָרעם.

מסתּמא שײַנט ס'געזיכט מײַנס אינעם חלום,
אַזש לאַניע גנבֿ ווערט אַ רודף־שלום,
לאַניע בײַ מײַן זײַט, מײַן שכן.

ער וועקט מיך שטילער, און ביז ווען איך וועק מיך
דערזע די וואָר און דערשרעק מיך,
פֿלאַנטערט זיך מײַן יום־טובֿ אין דער וואָכן...

Oh my poor grandfather, your bookcase
with its long dried-out Esrog from Sukes
still there, giving off fragrance —
and all the volumes scented:

The sun bestows a design of southerly light
upon the Talmud pages still open on the table,
which I left, deeply filled with wonder by its wisdom —
there was a man, and he turned to worm . . .

Perhaps my face glows in this dream
until even Leonye, the thief, becomes a man of peace,
Leonye, at my side, my neighbor.

He awakens me ever so gently and, fully aroused,
I perceive reality and become terrified,
my holiday entangled with a week day . . .

אָ, וויפֿל פֿעלט אַ מיש צו טאָן די בלעטער
און ס'איז אַזאַ מין שבתל בײַ טאָג,
דאָס שבתל, דאָס אײנציקס וואָס כ'פֿאַרמאָג,
און ווי דאָ – אַ ווינטיק שנייִיק וועטער.

שבת־אויפֿס גיט די באָבע שפּעטער:
– קינדערלעך, וואָס איז דאָס געיאָג?
„ברכי נפשי", דערוויַיל די באָבע זאָגט, –
שיט און שיט דער שניי אַן גאַנצע מעטערס.

בײַם ים פֿון שניי, ווי בײַ תּשליך, פֿון די טאַשן,
איך וואַרף די זינד און קען זיך נישט דערוואַשן:
– נאַ דיר אַלץ, נאָר גיב מיַין שבת אָפּ.

נאָר דער גזלן האָט אַלץ באַרויבט מיך קודם,
איך קלאַמער זיך אין אַבעס שטיבל־בוידעם,
נאָר ער וואַרפֿט פֿון דאָרט מיך אויך אַראָפּ...

O what would it take to be leafing through pages
on a homey little Shabes afternoon,
that precious Shabes, the only one I possess
and like here — windy, snowy weather.

Later grandmother gives us Shabes-fruit,
— "dear little children, what's the rush?"
she says, meanwhile reciting the "Bless My Soul" prayer,
and the snow pours and pours, complete meters.

As at Tashlekh, I throw the sins from my pockets
upon this sea of snow and cannot cleanse myself —
here, take everything, but return my Shabes!

Yet the bandit has already robbed me of it all;
I cling to the attic-roof of my grandmother's little hut,
and even from there, he hurls me down . . .

אַוודאַי איז אַ מאָל געוועזן יום-כיפור.
איז ערשט אויך, און פרעג מיר נישט קיין שאלות,
איך שטיי נאָך איצט אונטער זיידנס טלית
קוק פון דאָרט אַזש אַהער אַריבער.

אַזש ביז צו מיַין קלאָגלטאָג, מיַין טריבן.
ס'איז אַ טעות, מע דאַרף דאָך זאָגן „יעלות",
נאָר דער כאַם רעכנט אויס די מעלות
מיטן טמאָן פיסק, מיַינע זינד די זיבן.

כ'ענטפער נישט דער מיאוסער שלאָנג, דער הידרע,
מיַינע גלידער זינגען ערשט „כל נדרי"
און וואָס איז מיר מיַין בייזער בריגאַדיר?

ביז איך וועל צעהאַקן אַלע שטיינער,
וועל איך אין זיך שוין האַלטן ביַי עלינו,
אַ גוט-יאָר ווינטשן ייִדן ביַי דער טיר.

Certainly there was once Yonkiper
and now too, and I allow myself no scepticism.
I stand even now under my grandfather's prayer shawl
and look crosswise from right over there to here.

Right across to my dinky day of lament, this dreary day,
I've been in error! We must wail the prayer for forgiveness
though the boar reckons the merits of my seven sins
with his ritually impure snout.

I don't answer the ugly snake, the hydra;
now all the limbs of my body sing "Kol Nidre,"
and what do I care about this wicked brigadier?

By the time I have split every stone
I will have reached the final prayer
and wished Jews a good year at the door.

און ווער וועט מיר דעם וועג דען ערשט פֿאַרשפּאַרן
אַהין, אַהין וווּ כ'בין מיט מײַן „רמ״ח"?
ס'איז ווײַט דער וועג, און ס'קומט גיך אָן די נאַכט,
קיין קרעטשמער נישט, און נישט קיין אַרענדאַרן.

ס'אַ וויסט, ס'אַ וואַלד, סע ליעַרן געפֿאַרן
נאָר סע בליצט אַ ליכט, ערגעץ איז מען וואַך,
מ'האָט אַ טיר אין חושך אויפֿגעמאַכט,
און זע! ס'איז דאָך מײַן גוטער פֿעטער אַהרן!

וואָס טוט מײַן פֿעטער אַזוי שפּעט אין חצות?
ער לערנט תורה אַזוי־אַ ביז כעלות,
כ'הער נאָך קלאָר זײַן האַרציק זיסן ניגון.

אַז איך כאַפּ מיך אויף, איז אַלץ מיר גאָרנישט קלאָר:
אַ ליגן איז מײַן פֿינצטער־שווערע וואָר,
צי אפֿשר גאָר מײַן חלום איז אַ ליגן?...

28

Then who will block my path
to that place, that place where I am my innermost self?
The road is lengthy, and the night comes quickly,
but there is no innkeeper and no lessee in sight.

Such desolation, such a wilderness; what dangers lurk;
but a candle flashes; somewhere, someone's awake;
someone has opened a door into the darkness.
And look! It's my good Uncle Aaron, of course!

What's my Uncle doing up so late! He's studying Torah in this
         manner,
from midnight 'til the morning star ascends.
I still hear clearly his sweet, heart-felt melody . . .

Although when I wake up it's still not clear
whether my dark, burdensome reality is a lie,
or perhaps — is it possible! — my dream is entirely a lie . . .

האָט אָפּגעפֿאַסט אַ ייד אַ פֿערציק יאָרן
אויף גלות־שכינה און אַצינד געשיקט
זײַן בליק צו מיר.   אָ, ווי איז מיר, אַ בליק
אַז כ'בין פֿון אים פֿאַרציטערט אַזש געוואָרן.

זײַן פּנים ווערט נאָך ליטערער, נאָך קלאָרער.
עס קוקט מיך אָן דער צדיק, ר' מאיר יחיאל,
געשמועסט אַ מאָל אין לערנען, ער וויל
אויך איצט מיר זאָגן וואָס מע טאָר נישט.

אָ, משפּט מײַן נשמה מיט טויזנט טויטן,
און לייג מיך, לייג מיך בײַ די פּליטן,
כ'בין אין גאַנצן דײַן, אַ הייליקער ייד!

מײַן באָבע האָט אַ מאָל געריסן קבֿרים
אין מײַן קרענק, נאָר איצטער בין איך אָרעם
ווען סע גליט אין פֿיבער מײַן געמיט.

A Jew who fasted some forty years
because of the exile of the Divine Presence
now casts his glance. O woe is me, a piercing glance
that paralyzes with fear!

His face becomes still purer, clearer,
he scrutinizes me, this holy Reb Meyer Yekhiel
with whom I spoke once about my studies.
Even now, he wants to tell me what is forbidden!

Oh try my soul with a thousand deaths
and lay me down, lay me down near the fence,
I am all yours, O holy Jew!

When I was ill, my grandmother wailed
enough to tear the ancestors from their graves,
but now, when my spirit glows with fever,
I am bereft!

... און מעשׂיות הערן אין מלװה-מלכה-נעכט,

און איך בין אַ שאָטן אין װינקל אײַנגעהערט,

און מײַנע ייִדן זײַנען שטיקער הימל אױף דער ערד,

ייִדן װי בײַ מערזערן אױפֿן בלעך.

און די לבֿנה גלײַך פֿון צוװײַגן װי אַן עפּל מען ברעכט

און מיט קפֿיצת-הדרך פֿליִען פֿערד

אַהין װוּ דער װוּנדער איז באַשערט,

דער צדיק פֿירט מיטן שטן ערשט געפֿעכט.

פֿאַר װאָס געשעט קײן װוּנדער, גאָט, נישט מער?

אַלע נעכט האָסטו געברענגט אַהער,

פֿון גאַנצער װעלט און דאָ זײ אױסגעצױגן.

די לבֿנה זיך גנבֿעט אין אַ זײַט

און איז װי קײן מאָל אַזױ װײַט

און שעמט זיך צו קוקן אין די אױגן.

. . . and to hear wonder-stories at Melave Malke nights:
and I am a spellbound shadow in a corner,
and my Jews are pieces-of-heaven on the earth,
Jews being shaped by these tales
as if in a tin vessel pounded by a brass pestle.

And the moon, as though of the branches, is an apple you break,
and the horses jump the road, and fly
to that place where wonder is predestined —
now the saintly man is struggling with Satan.

God, why don't wonders happen any more?
You have brought all the nights here
from the whole world, and from the first stretched them out.

The moon slips away;
it has never been so distant,
so shy of my eye.

חלומען זיך מיר ספֿרים ייִדישע מיט ר״שי־כּתבֿ,
פֿאַרגעלטע בלעטער דפֿוס אַמסטערדאַם,
אַ ירושה פֿון אַן עלטער־זיידן מן־הסתּם,
אַ צדיק־מפֿורסם, אַ רבֿ בן־הרבֿ.

און איך בלעטער אַזוי כּסדר דף נאָך דף:
,,ודע – און ווייס בן־אָדם, אַז אין יעדן פֿלאַם
ליִערן די קליפֿות פֿון דעם ס״ם,
אין גוטס און שלעכטס פֿאַרמישט דאָס גאַנץ באַשאַף.

און די וואָס ווערן פֿון זינד נישט זאַט,
ווערן שפּעטער מגולגל אין אַ בלאַט
אויף אַ בוים געוואָרפֿן פֿונעם ווינט.

דאַרף מען נאָך אָפֿקומען די זינד?
דער בלאַט איז שוין אָפֿגעפֿליקט פֿון בוים,
ליגט אין רינשטאָק און באַוועגט זיך קוים.

I dream of Jewish sacred books with Rashi-script,
yellowed pages printed in Amsterdam,
perhaps an inheritance from my great-grandfather,
a renowned Tsadek, a rabbi, a rabbi's son,

and so, I leaf through page after page:
"and know — and know son-of-man," that in each flame
lurk shards of evil
and good and evil are mixed through all of creation;

and those who are not sated by sin
are transmuted into the leaves
of a tree, tossed away by the wind.

Must we still suffer this sin?
The leaf has been plucked from the tree;
it lies in the gutter, barely moving.

װי זאָגט ר' אַבֿרהם חיים: אין גיהנום איז אױך דאָ גאָט,
טײלט ער ייִדן איבערגעשריבענע קאַפּיטלעך תהלים,
װיַיל מע דאַרף דאָך זיַין בלינד נישט צו זען אים פֿאַרהילן
און אין אַכזריות נישט דערקענען זיַין גענאָד.

נישטאָ קיין פּשט אױף דער װעלט, ס'איז כּולו־סוד,
אַז סע פֿײַניקט זיך אַ מענטש ברענגען גװילים
נאָר ייִדן קענען זינגען „שבֿח גאולים"
אַפֿילו װען באַלאַגערט איז די שטאָט.

ס'איז כּולו־חייבֿ, די װעלט זי ליגט אין תהום,
נאָר ר' אַבֿרהם חיים זוכט װי אַ מאָל אין סדום
די גערעכטע פֿופֿציק צו געבן װעלט אַ תיקון,

ביז װאָס־װען טרײַבט מען צום „אַפּיל",
און װעכטער שרײַצן, און די הינט עס בילן,
עס פֿעלן צום חשבון אפֿשר די צדיקים?...

36

Thus says Reb Avrom Khaim as he distributes copied verses of
          psalms to Jews:
"There is also a God in Gehenem — ," because you'd have to be blind
not to see him enveloping us
and in the midst of cruelty not recognize his mercy.

There is no simple meaning to the world; all of it is mystery;
when a truly pious man is tortured, parchment burns,
but Jews can intone "Let the Redeemer Sing Praises"
even when The City is besieged.

We're all guilty; the world lies in abyss,
but as of old in Sodom, Reb Avrom Khaim
seeks the righteous fifty to repair the world.

Before you know it, you're driven to the "roll call";
guards yell, dogs bark —
Could it be the saints are missing from the reckoning . . . ?

און ר' אברהם חיים שרײַט: „נישט פֿאַרגעס,
האָסט אַ זיידן געהאַט דעם הייליקן ייִד,
בינד זיך אָן אין אים, ער ציט
אַרויס דיר פֿון שערי־טומאה די מים־טיח."

בײַ אַ ייִדן אין אַ תפֿילה דער מעת־לעת:
דער פֿרימאָרגן – אַ קאַפֿיטל תהלים אין געמיט,
און נעילה – דער פֿאַרנאַכט און רויט צעגליט,
און אין בײַטאָג – אַ משל אַלץ וואָס זעסט.

און אַ ווײַסער קיטל ווערט דאָס פֿעלד מיט שניי,
אין סיבירער לאַגער שטייען ייִדן צוויי,
מע רעדט און מע דערררעדט זיך צום בעל־שם,

ביז שפּעט אַזוי, ביז דניעװאַלני שרײַט „אָטבאַי!"
און ס'איז אַלץ אַ משל, אויך דער פֿרעמדער גױ,
און פֿרעמדער ווערט נאָך אַלץ וואָס איז די פֿרעמד.

38

And Reb Avrom Khaim cries: don't forget
you had a grandfather, that holy Jew,
bind yourself to him; he pulls you
out of the forty-nine gates of uncleanliness.

A Jew's twenty-four hour period in prayer:
morning — with its mood intimate as a psalm;
the Nila — at dusk's red glow,
and during the day — parables in all one sees . . .

and the field of snow is transformed into a kitel . . .
In a Siberian labor camp two Jews stand;
they talk and talk, 'til they reach the topic of the Bal Shem Tov,

when the soldier on duty yells "break it up!"
and everything becomes a parable, even the strange gentile —
and all the strangeness becomes stranger still.

משה בראָדערזאָן וויקלט זיך באנדאַזשן אויף די וווּנדן זײַנע וויצן
און ר' אַבֿרהם חיים זאָגט: אַז דו ווילסט איז גאָר אַ זכות
מגולגל ווערן אין סיביר, פֿון טומאה דער רשות,
ווײַל דו ווייסט דען וויפֿל ס'בעטן זיך ניצוצות.

הײַליקע, פֿון שלעכטס ארויס נעם און באַשיץ אונדז,
און מיט עמערס שעפּסטו אונטער יעדער קוסט,
בײַמי בעל-שם האָט מען ס'אָרט דאָ נישט געוווּסט,
ער וואָלט אַהער געלאָפֿן מיט דרך-קפֿיצות.

פֿון מעזשיביזש ביז לענאַ מי יודע ווי ס'איז ווײַט,
ר' אַבֿרהם חיים דערנענטערט דעם שטח און די צײַט,
כאָטש גרויזאַם פֿאַרקטיק לאָזט אַראָפּ זיך סיבירער דעמער

הערסטו אַ מעשׂה: דער בעל-שם פֿלעגט פֿאָרן אויף יאַרידים
מתקן זײַן נשמות און דו ביסט אַ חסיד פֿון חסידים,
און דער ווינט ווערט אַ זמר.

Moyshe Broderson wraps his jokes like bandages on wounds,
and Reb Avrom Khaim says: if you wish it's really a rare
            privilege
to wind up in Siberia's spiritually unclean domain,
because do you know how much the holy sparks beseech us?

Holy ones deliver us from evil, protect us —
here there is so much evil one scoops it up with pails under
            every bush!
In the days of the Bal Shem this place was unheard of,
or he'd have leaped here with miraculous short cuts.

Who knows how far it is from Mezhibezh to Lena?
Reb Avrom Khaim brings time and distance closer,
although the dreadful Siberian dusk savagely descends.

You know something — the miracle worker used to travel to fairs
            by wagon
in order to save souls; and you are a Hosed of Hasidism,
and the wind becomes a Hasidic song.

וילבש קללה כמדו...
(תהלים)

מיַן גאָט, איך גלייב דיר אזוי פֿיל,
גלייב מיר אויך אַ ביסל...
האָסט מיך געשאָלטן מיט אזוי פֿיל פֿרווו,
שטאַרק מיר דאָס געוויסן.

כ'האָב אָנגעטאָן די קללה אויף זיך
און סע סטאַרטשען אַרויס די גלידער,
גיב לויט מיַן מאָס צו שטייגן אין דער הייך
און צו פֿאַלן אין דער נידער.

צווישן דיַן באַשאַף וויל איך נישט זיַן גרויס,
נאָר אויך נישט זיַן דער קלענסטער,
דיַן גרויסע זון שענקט דאָך בלויז אַ שטראַל
אין קליינע טורמע-פֿענצטער.

האָסט מיך געמאַכט פֿאַר דיַן הייליקער,
לאָז מיך נישט ווערן דיַן פֿאַרשוועכער,
האָסט דאָך אַ מאָס געגעבן אַפֿילו דעם קאָליר
אינעם בלומען-בעכער.

און מיט אזוי פֿיל פֿינצטערערניש געשטראָמט די נאַכט
זי זאָל זיך נישט איבערשימען,
און אַז דו האָסט דעם ים פֿאַרשאָלטן מיט ווילדערניש
האָסטו דאָך אים אויך געטאָן מיט אַ ברעג צוימען.

He will wear the curse according to his measure . . .
Psalm 109, verses 18, 19

My God I believe in you so much,
believe in me too a little.
You have cursed me with so many tests,
strengthen my conscience.

I've dressed myself in the curse
and my limbs protrude.
Whether I rise or fall
only meter out what I can measure up to.

Neither do I want to be your main
nor your most minor creation.
Even your great sun still gifts me with a ray
through my tiny prison window.

You have made me your holy one;
don't let me become your desecrator.
Indeed you've even bestowed a measure of color
to the flower's calyx.

Though you punished the night
with such darkness — you contained it.
Though you cursed the sea with wildness,
the shore restrains it.

א תפילה פון א מענטשן אין שניי

ס'איז היַנט קיַין בלוטפלעק נישטאָ אין שניי,
מ'האָט קיַינעם נישט געשאָסן, איז שניי און שניי.
אַרום דיר – שניי,
אין דיר – שניי,
וויַיס צו וויַיס.

אַ, באַהיט מיך, גאָט, פון די שנייַיקע ווערטער:
מנא מנא תקל ופרסין.
פאַרן דאַרפיש פנים: שניי
פאַרן הימל וואָס האָט נישט וווּ צו פאַלן
און פאַלט אין שניי,
פאַר טויערלעך צעוויגטע אין ווינט
וואָס האָבן אַזוי פיל צו זאָגן
און זאָגן בלויז: שניי
פאַרן דאַרפיש פנים: שניי,
פאַר שחרית – שניי, מוסף – שניי, מעריב – שניי,
פאַר מיזרח, מערב, צפון, דרום – שניי,
אַ מענטש אין שניי,
אַ הונט אין שניי,
אַ פערד אין שניי.

דאָס טאָגל צײלט ווי אַ קינד
ביז צוויי:
אײנס – שניי,
צוויי – שניי,
שניי,
שניי.

PRAYER OF A MAN IN SNOW

Today there is no bloodstain on the snow;
no one was shot; there's just snow and snow
around you — snow
in you snow — white on white.

O protect me God, from snowy Words:
You have been weighed and found wanting.
God has numbered thy kingdom and finished it.
The face of the village: snow.
The sky that has nowhere to fall —
and sinks into snow.
The little gates swinging in the wind —
so much to say and only saying: snow.
For the village face — snow;
for morning prayers — snow, added prayers — snow, sunset
        prayers — snow,
for east, west, north, south — snow,
a man in snow
a dog in snow
a horse in snow.

This precious little day counts like a child
up to two:
one — snow
two — snow,
snow,
snow.

אַגינסקיס פּאָלאָנעז אין סיביר

ביז פֿופֿציק גראַד די פֿראָסטיק שטײַפֿע טעג,
וווּ וועסטו זיך אַהינטאָן, מײַן דינער, וויכער ניגון?
דאָ לאָזן זיך בעריאָזעס נישט פֿאַרוויגן,
זיי גליווערן מיט שניי, פֿאַרשטיט בײַם וועג.

מיט דײַן פּאָלאָנעז אין ברוסט ווי אַ פֿאַרמעג,
און ראַדיאָ-קלאַנגען וואַרעמען אָן דעם שטח,
איך וועל אַרויס אַ זיגער פֿון געוועט איצט,
נאָך פֿאַרן קלאַנג דערגרייכן כ'וועל דעם ברעג.

בײַם ברעג אין האַרבסט, ס'פֿאַלן נאָך געלע בלעטער,
און אַ האַנט איז דאָ וואָס צײלט זיי איבער שפּעטער,
און יעדער בלאַט איז אַ ליבעבריוו אין טרויער.

מײַן קינדהייט בלאָנקעט דאָרט אויף טויִקער פּאָליאַנע,
נישט פֿאַרשטײענדיק, זי האָט טיף אַזוי פֿאַרשטאָנען
און בענקט, ווי דו, בײַם פֿאַרמאַכטן טויער.

OGINSKI'S POLONAISE IN SIBERIA

Days frozen stiff, as low as fifty below;
where will you find a home, my thin soft melody?
Birch trees along the road are so rigid with snow
they can't let themselves be swayed to sleep.

Possessed within my breast by your Polonaise,
even this vastness is warmed by radio sounds;
now I can win the bet,
I can reach the camp's edge before the sound dissipates . . .

Beyond the boundary it is autumn; yellow leaves are still falling,
and later a hand will count them —
each leaf a sorrowful love letter.

My childhood looses itself in this glistening glade,
not grasping what it has so deeply understood,
and, like you, yearns at the locked Gate.

תּפֿילה

גאָט, גאָט, גיב אַ רעגן
פֿאַר די קליינע קינדערס וועגן...
(פֿון אַ פֿאָלקסליד)

גאָט, גאָט, גיב נישט קיין רעגן,
פֿאַר די גרויסע קינדערס וועגן,
דער רעגן, דער רעגן איז נישט געבעטנשט,
ווען ס'וויקט זיך אין בלאָטע און סע שטינקט דײַן מענטש.

דײַן מענטש, דײַן מענטש איז פֿאָרט עפּעס דאָך,
אָן אים איז פֿרײד נישט קיין פֿרייד און בראָך נישט קיין בראָך,
און וויפֿל קומט אָן מיט דער גרינער גאַל
צו פּוצן און פּוצן דעם גאַנצן וועלטל,
זיך אויסגעשפּיגלט און דו ביסט אַזוי שײן,
ווייס דאָך אויך בלויז דערפֿון דײַן מענטש אַליין,
ווײַל בעל־חי איז נאַריש און קריכט פֿון דער הויט,
פֿאַר דײַן קנעכט אַפֿילו, דײַן שׂטן, דעם טויט:
סע צעבילן זיך הינט אין שטאָט אויף דער קייט,
און דער הענער זיך וועקן פֿאַרטאָגיק צעקרייט,
אַ נאַרישע שׂימחה אויף זײַערע קעפּ,
ווען פֿרעמדער פֿאַרצײַט דאָ שואָרצענעם קרעפּ
אויף הײַזער, אויף גאַסן פֿון שטאָט אין דער פֿרי,
יענער, דער פֿרעמדער, דער גאַסט פֿון נישט־הי.
נאָר מענטש, דײַן מענטש, ווייס אײַנער אַליין,
דײַן הינק אין אַ צװיג װאָס וויגט זיך, דײַן מיין,
דײַן אָפֿענע שפּראַך אין טאָג װען דו באַוווּזט
ווי אויף דער האַנט אַלץ און אין נעכט װען דו שװײַגסט,
און װאָס איז אָפֿן געוווֹזן װערט פֿאַרבאָהאַלטענער סוד,
טאָ פֿאַרשעם נישט דײַן מענטש, דײַן צירונג, מײַן גאָט.

PRAYER

God, God give a rain for
the sake of the little
children . .
    (from a folksong)

God, God don't give any rain
for the sake of the big children,
the rain, the rain is not blessed
when it soaks into mud and stinks up man.

Your human being, your own human being, is, after all, still worth
          something!
Without them joy isn't joy, disaster isn't disaster.
Though you polish the whole world
with spit from the green gall of your guts,
until all is so exquisite and beautiful,
only man alone is aware of it.
Because the serpent is foolish and crawls out of its skin,
for us your servants, your very shadow, you have metered out death:
In town dogs tied to chains begin to bark,
and roosters awake at dawn crowing,
with foolish celebrations on their heads,
as they harken in the morning
to a stranger on the city streets
who shrouds houses in black crepe
when death, that foreigner, that out-of-town guest appears.
But only human beings, your human beings, can comprehend
your wink in a nodding branch, your every intent,
for the language of your day is as open as a hand,
and your night as closed as the silence of hidden secrets.
My God, don't put to shame your very own human being, your jewels!

הימן צום זונען־אונטערגאַנג אין סיביר

Smutno mi Boże...
(Slowacki)

איז מיר אומעטיק, מײַן גאָט, וואָס די שקיעה איז דאָ אַזוי שײן,
מיט אַזוי פֿיל פֿאַרבן, אַזוי פֿיל פֿאַרבן,
אויף דײַן הימל – אַזוי שײן און אונטן – אַזוי מיאוס
מענטשן שטאַרבן...
איז מיר אומעטיק, מײַן גאָט...

ביסט אַוועק, אַוועק, און פֿאַרבעטן פֿײגל אין דער ווײַט
ווי צו אַ חתונה, צו אַ שׂימחה־פֿלאַקער,
ווי אַ פֿײער וואָס לויפֿט אַוועק און לאָזט איבער זײַן פֿעלד
אין ברען פֿון פֿאַרזײ, זײַן פֿעלד נישט געאַקערט –
איז מיר אומעטיק, מײַן גאָט...

אָ, אַנטפּלעק מיר דעם שליסל צו דײַן פֿאַרבאַרגענער שטאָט,
כ'וויל וויסן דעם זין פֿון דײַן משפּט, דעם האַרבן,
פֿאַר וואָס אַלץ בײַ דיר אויבן איז אַזוי וווּנדערלעך שײן
און אונטן אַזוי מיאוס וועלן מענטשן שטאַרבן –
איז מיר אומעטיק, מײַן גאָט...

HYMN TO SUNSET IN SIBERIA

My God I am Sad . . .
— Slowacki

My God I am sad; the sunset here is so beautiful,
with so many, many colors!
Above such beauty, and below such ugliness,
and people dying . . .
My God I am sad . . .

Like a peasant who abandons his fields
for a wedding or torch-light festival
at the height of sowing, leaving the land unplowed,
you've gone far away, and lured the birds aloft —
My God I am sad . . .

Oh reveal the key to your hidden city.
Tell me the point of your harsh judgment.
Oh why is everything so wondrously lovely above with you,
while here below it's so ugly that people die?
My God I am sad . . .

א תפילה פֿאַרן שװאַכן

אָן דעם שװאַכן – אַ, העלף אים, העלף אים, גאָט,
ער זאָל צו אַ מענטש זײַן געגליכן,
ס'האָט אים באַשפֿיגן די װעלט, זאָל ער צו דיר
אויף אַלע פֿיר כאָטש דערקריכן.

דײַן אייביקייט גרייט אָן די װעלט
פֿאַרן העלד, דער שװאַכער האָט דײַנע מינוטן געװאָלט נאַשן
און איז געבליבן װי אויף אַ יאַריד
אַ באַגנבֿעטער ייִד, מיט ליידיקע טאַשן.

ביסט אַלמעכטיק און טראָגסט אויס אויף זיך
די מאַסע, די שװערע פֿון װעלטן און שטערן,
נאָר דער פֿאַרנאַכט איז דאָך אויך דײַנער, דײַן שװאַכע מינוט,
װען דײַן הימל עס גליט פֿון בענקשאַפֿט און באַגערן.

טאָ העלף אים, דעם שװאַכן, העלף אים, גאָט,
ער זאָל צו אַ מענטש זײַן געגליכן,
ס'האָט אים באַשפֿיגן די װעלט, טאָ זאָל ער צו דיר
אויף אַלע פֿיר כאָטש דערקריכן...

A PRAYER FOR THE FRAIL ONE

And the weak one — oh help him, help him God
to equal a human being;
though the world has spat on him, at least,
crawling on all fours, he should be able to reach you.

Your everlastingness prepares the world for heroes,
while the weak one who wanted to nibble your minutes
is left with empty pockets,
like a Jew robbed at a fair.

You are almighty and bear upon you
the weighty mass of worlds and stars
but certainly evening, when the sky glows
with longing and yearning, is your weak moment.

Then help him, the weak one, help him, God,
to equal a human being;
though the world has spat on him, at least,
crawling on all fours, he should be able to reach you.

אויסגעחלומט שטיללעבן

אַ גלאָז טיי,
אַ שיינע, ריינע גלאָז טיי,
אַ היימישע, אַ שמעקנדיק זיסע,
אין דין געשליפן גלאָז
אויף אַ שטילן טיש,
באַדעקט מיט ווייס,

אין דער ליכטיקער שטוב,
אַ צייטונג מיט נייַס,
אַ וואַזאָן ליידיקגיין,
גאָרנישט טאָן מאָרגן.
איך טרינק פאַמעלעך, פאַמעלעך
דעם כּוס
און רייכער
אַ געשמאַקן פּאַפּיראָס.

DREAMED UP STILL-LIFE

A glass of tea,
a lovely, clear glass of tea
dear, sweet smelling,
in thinly polished glass
on a peaceful table,
covered with white,

in the sunlit house.
A newspaper with news,
a loafing plant,
nothing to do tomorrow.
Slowly, slowly I drink
the glass
and smoke
a delicious cigarette.

כ'װעל טוישן דאָס ברויט אויף אַ קעסטעלע טאַבאַק,
געװײנט שוין, געװײנט שוין צו אַ טאָג אָן ברויט,
װאָס זאָל איך טאָן? -- אין מעבר יבק
זעט זיך נישט פֿאַר אַזאַ מין אַ טויט.

דערעסן דאָס אייביקע אין ריי גיין, אין ריי גיין,
און ס'איז גאָר אַ ברכה: מיט די פֿיס צום טיר,
אַז כ'האָב שוין פֿאַרגעסן צי דאַרף איך אויף צװיי גיין,
צי גאָר, װי אַ בהמה, קריכן אויף פֿיר...

I will trade the bread for a small box of tobacco,
already accustomed, already resigned to a day without bread;
what shall I do? — even in the Yabbok
such a death, such woe, couldn't be read.

Fed up, the everlasting march in a line, march in a line,
and it's a blessing to be dead, with your feet to the door;
I have already forgotten if I have to walk on two all the time
or completely crawl like a beast on all fours.

צי מיט מיר, צי אָן מיר,
וועלן טעג אויסגיין מיט אַ טויט, אַ האַרבן,
און בעריאָזקעס וועלן אַרומגיין און זוכן זייער פֿאַרלוירענע בענקשאַפֿט
און וויינען זוכנדיק.

און שטיינער וועלן זאָגן אַ סוף, אַן עק, פֿאַרפֿאַלן,
און שווייגן,
נאָר פֿייגל וועלן שטורעמען די הימלען און מאַכן סקאַנדאַלן
אויך צוזייגן.

און גראָזן, וואָס האָבן זיך באַגנוגנט וואָקסן ביי דער סאַמער ערד,
וועלן זאָגן: פֿאָטערל – טו מיט אונדז וואָס דו ווילסט,
נאָר נישט שטאַרבן.
ס'וועלן זיי אויפֿעסן די פֿערד,
נאָר די פֿערד וועלן אויך שטאַרבן.

און איך וועל וועל זיין אַ בלום דעמאָלט, צי עפּעס אַנדערש וואָס,
אין וועלכע די אַרבעטזאַמע ערד וועט מיין געבוין פֿאַרוואַנדלען,
די צייַט – די זשומענדיקע בין
וועט מיר אויסנאָגן דעם האָניק און די פֿאַרבן
פֿאַר דער אייביקייט,
איך וועל אַ בלום זיין
און ווידער שטאַרבן.
און מענטשן וואָס וועלן דעמאָלט זיין?
זיי וועלן מסתמא טאָן דאָס און יענץ,
און אַז זיי וועלן נישט האָבן וואָס צו טאָן,
וועלן זיי זיך קוילען און שטאַרבן,
אָדער גלאָט אַזוי שטאַרבן –
אַ געשעפֿט צו שטאַרבן?

58

With or without me
days will pass to their harsh death,
and birches will be transplanted and search for their lost longing
and weep as they're yearning.

And the rocks shall foretell: an end,
that's it, it's lost,
and say no more;
but birds will storm the sky and scandalize the branches.

And grasses satisfied to grow by the very earth
will plead: dear little father — do what you will
but don't let us die.
The horses will eat the blades of grass,
but the horses too will die.

I will be a flower then, or perhaps something else,
into which the industrious earth will have transformed my bones;
time — that buzzing bee
will draw out the honey and color
for eternity.
I will be a flower
and die again,
and the people that will then be?
Perhaps they will do this and that,
and when they've nothing better to do,
they will slit each other's throat and die,
or just die —
it's no big deal to die.

און ערשט איז שוין גוט, די ביינער, די דּאַרע,
באָדן זיך אויס אין וויכן געלעגער,
נאָר נישט איין מאָל כ'פיל זיך אַן אַרעסטאַנט אויף דער נּאַרע
און הער דעם „שטיי אויף" נאָך אַלץ פֿונעם וועקער.

און כ'צי פֿון געוווינשאַפֿט צום דיל נאָך די קליידער,
ס'וועט וואָרטן אַ פֿריריקער דרויסן, אַ גראָוער,
ווען וואַלד און וועג און קופקעלע היַזער,
איז איין טונקעלער פֿלעק אויף עפּעס אַ טאָוול.

And now it's already pretty good; my bones, my emaciated bones
bathe in a soft bed;
yet frequently I feel like a prisoner on a plank cot,
and hear the waker's "get up" call

and automatically pull up my clothes from the floor
to await a frosty outdoors, a gray day
when the forests, and the roads, and the little cluster of houses
are all one dark splotch on some kind of canvas.

מײַן שטעטל

אּון װעּן אּיך װעּל אַהין דעּרגײן,
װעּט זיכער שוין דאָס הויז נישט שטײן,
אּון בלײַבן װעּט צו טאָן אַ װײן
װי אַ מאָל, אַ מאָל אַ קינד.

אּון װי אַ מאָל אּין מאַמעּס שויס
די מעשׂה אירע לאָזט זיך אויס:
– געװעּן אַ מאָל, געװעּן אַ הויז,
נישטאָ, נישטאָ אַצינד.

אּון צװישן ציגל, הויפֿנס אַש,
רויִנען־גראַז אּון קויט אּון סאַזש,
פֿאַרגאַנגענהײט װעּט טאָן אַ טאַש
דעּר װינט.

נאָר װאָס געװעּן װעּט זײַן שוין װײַט,
אַזוי װײַט פֿאַר נײַער צײַט,
נײַע צײַט אּון נײַע לײַט –
דאָס מעשׂהלע פֿאַרשװינדט.

(סיביר, אין לאַגער)

MY TOWN

. . . And when I reach there,
surely the house will no longer stand where it was.
All that'll be left to do is stare, and cry
like I sometimes did as a child, long long ago . . .

and sometimes, just as then, on mother's lap,
her story ends with a gap:
— Once upon a time, there was a house, perhaps
now there isn't, oh there isn't no!

Amidst bricks and piles of ashes,
dirt and soot and wild grasses,
the wind will have trashed the past
I used to know,

for what was will now be long-gone,
far too distant for a new-age song;
new-time's wrongs, newly respectable throngs--
and the little tale disappears, just so . . .

[Siberia, in labor camp]

פֿאַר פֿרילינג

וויליק, צי אפֿשר נישט וויליק,
אַזוי וויַיט דעם האַרץ און פֿרעמד
פֿאַרן ליכטיק צעשמייכלטן פֿרילינג
עס האָט מײַן געמיט זיך פֿאַרשעמט.

ס'איז אַזוי פֿיל פֿאַרבײַ און קומט נאָך
נאָר אין מיר — — װי שטיל איז; װי שטיל!
אַמאָליק אַזוי עס ברומט נאָך,
װי אַ טויב, דער יונגער אַפּריל.

ס'איז ערגעץ פֿאַרפֿרוירן מײַן חלום
אין װינטערס אויף שניי און אויף אײַז,
ערשט ציִען װינטלעך בײַ פּאָלעס,
װי קינדער אַן אַלטיקן גרײַז.

זיי װעלן אים ערגעץ דערפֿרירן,
אויף װעגן װער װייס װוּהין,
אין װעלדער אים ערגעץ פֿאַרלירן
בײַ פֿייגל, בײַ ביימער, בײַ גרינס...

BEFORE SPRING

Willingly, perhaps unwillingly,
despite my alienated and remote heart,
spring's suffusing smile
shames my spirits.

So much has passed and is still to come,
but within me how quiet it is, so quiet
at times young April hums
like a dove!

Somewhere, my dream is frozen
in a winter of snow and ice,
but how these breezes tug at the flaps of my overcoat,
like children urging on a frosty-haired elder.

They will lead him somewhere,
on who knows what paths,
and there lose him in the fields
among trees, among birds, among meadows.

NOTES

p. 19

H. Lang--an unknown reference.

l. 8 "fourth on the ground"--it was not uncommon for people to share beds, alternating during the night.

----

p. 21

l. 6 Khalemoyed--the four days between the first two and last two days of Pesach.

----

p. 23

l. 2 Sukes--the fall harvest holiday. Esrog is the fruit of the citroen used with the palm branch at Sukes.

l. 11 Leonye--a gentile murderer of five who slept next to Emiot and was "rehabilitated" by the Jewish and/or political prisoners. When drunk, he reverted and hid a butcher knife in his boot. Emiot would watch and remove the knife when possible.

----

p. 25

l. 9 Tashlekh--the first day of Rosheshone, tne New Year, when people go to the river and cast crumbs from their pockets to symbolize their sins.

----

p.27

l. 8 "impure snout"--Jews referred to parts of gentile bodies with animal parts.

l. 10 Kol Nidre--Aramaic prayer chanted prior to sunset on the eve of Yonkiper which has come to symbolize tragedy, suffering, collective sins, and repentance.

l. 13 "final prayer"--obliging us to praise God for all of Creation, choosing the Jewish people, and anticipating the day when understanding will be complete.

----

p. 29

l. 2 "innermost self"--literally, organs, limbs. There are 248 commandments and 248 parts of the body.

l. 9 "studying Torah in this manner"--during Shavues, the entire night may be spent reciting special excerpts from the Torah and rabbinic law.

----

p. 31

l. 6 Reb Meyer Yekhiel--the famous Rabbi from Ostrow, a genius and pious Tsadek who fasted 40 years because of the exile of the Divine Presence.

l. 10 "near the fence"--transgressors were buried by the fence.

l. 12 "wailed"--old Orthodox custom, to implore ancestors to intercede on behalf of the sick.

----

p. 33

l. 1 "Melave Malke"--literally: to escort the Queen. Hasidic ceremony at the end of Sabbath to escort the spirit of Sabbath out the door.

----

p. 35

l. 1 "Rashi-script"--Rashi was a great 11th century commentator who lived in France.

l. 3 great-grandfather--Emiot was descended on his mother's side from the Yid Ha-Kodesh, "The Holy Jew," a famous Hasidic master in 19th century Poland.

l. 4 Tsadek--saintly man

l. 6 See Ezekiel, chapter 37.

----

p. 37

l. 1 "Reb Avrom Khaim, a Lubavitch Hasid from Samerkand, who was imprisoned together with us." (Footnote by Emiot)

l. 6 "parchment burns"--Rabbi Akiba (70A.D.) was caught studying Torah by the Romans, wrapped in Torah parchment, and burned at the stake, saying, "the parchment is burning but the letters are rising to the heavens."

----

p. 39

l. 4 There are 49 levels of impurity. Jews in Egypt were on the 49th. At the 50th you die. Also 49 levels of wisdom balance this.

l. 7 Nila--prayer recited on Yonkiper asking God's forgiveness.

l. 9 "kitel"--white linen robe worn by Rabbi on Yonkiper.

l. 11 Bal Shem Tov--founder of Hasidism, miracle worker.

----

p. 41

l. 1 Moyshe Broderson--A Jewish writer Emiot knew in Poland. He was not imprisoned until 1950. Emiot credits Broderson's personality and ability to care for others with greatly helping him survive the camps.

l. 4 "holy sparks"--Hasidim believed the holy sparks of creation are imprisoned until Jews release them by prayer.

l. 9 The Lena River, in central Asia, flows NE to the Arctic Ocean.

----

p. 43

l. 16 "calyx"--literally: wine cup.

----

p. 45

lines 6-7--Literally an acrostic from the Book of Daniel.

----

p. 47

title--Oginski, 1765-1833, was (and still is) a popular Polish composer.

----

p. 51

epigraph--Slowacki was a major 19th century Polish romantic poet. Emiot's poem is inspired by "Smutno mi Boże" written while Slowacki was exiled at sea. To this day, Poles regard this poem as part of their national identity.

----

p. 57

l. 3 "Yabbok"--*Prayers for Sick*, Amsterdam, 1752, book containing prayers for the sick and dying.

----

p. 59

lines 3-4--Russian birches are of the variety known as "weeping white birches." They grow in clusters or pairs and rarely survive in Siberia.

----

p. 65

l. 12 "elder"--Yiddish for "old man" and "mistake" are the same word (*grayz*).

The NIGHT the ANGELS SANG

and three other dramas for Christmas

Abingdon Press
Nashville

The Night the Angels Sang

ISBN 0-687-05467-2

06 07 08 09 10 11 12 13 - 10 9 8 7 6 5 4 3 2

Manufactured in the United States of America

CONTENTS

The Night the Angels Sang 5

The Christmas Card 9

Get Back in Your Box 17

The Jazzy, Snazzy Shepherd Boy 25

THE NIGHT THE ANGELS SANG
Adapted from a story by Leigh Gregg

Production Notes
*Stage should be divided into two parts: the hills surrounding
Bethlehem and the stable. Use lights to show the different
parts. Depending on your layout, you may want the shepherds
to go out into the auditorium or sanctuary and come back to
the stage when they hurry to Bethlehem, or go straight across
the stage to the stable while the angel chorus sings.*

Make the set as simple or as elaborate as you wish.

Characters
Speaking roles:
Shepherds (use as many as seven or as few as two)
Angel chorus or choir

Nonspeaking roles:
Mary and Joseph
Extra shepherds, if you have a lot of children

Props
You will need a stable, or at least a manger with the baby
(baby can be represented by a light in the manger).
Shepherds should have a fire made of crumpled red tis-
sue paper and sticks, lit by a flashlight. They should turn
the flashlight off before going to the stable.

All characters should be in typical biblical dress; shep-
herds should carry staffs. Choir or angel chorus can be
dressed as angels.

Scene One

(*The scene opens with the* SHEPHERDS *gathered around their campfire. Some should actually be asleep, while others are keeping watch. The* ANGEL CHORUS *or* CHOIR *sings the first verse of* "While Shepherds Watched Their Flocks by Night." *The* CHOIR *should not be lighted at this time.*)

SHEPHERD 1: Let me tell you about what happened one evening out on the hillside. My brothers and I had all the sheep settled down for the night. Just as we were beginning to get drowsy ourselves, something strange happened. The sky filled with a great light, and an angel of the Lord appeared to us.

(*Light comes up on one* ANGEL.)

SHEPHERD 1: The night became so bright, it was like daytime. I was afraid it would frighten the sheep. It certainly frightened me!

SHEPHERD 2: The angel told us not to be afraid, but we were scared. You would be too! But the angel said there was good news for us. Our Savior had been born! Then the whole sky was filled with angels singing, "Glory to God in the highest heaven, and on earth peace among those whom He favors."

(*Light comes up on* CHOIR *or* ANGEL CHORUS. CHORUS *or* CHOIR *sings verses two through four of* "While Shepherds Watched Their Flocks by Night.")

Shepherd 3: This angel chorus was the very first Christmas carol. No more beautiful song was ever heard before or will be heard again. It was in this song that the angels announced the birth of the Savior of the world.

(CHORUS *or* CHOIR *sings "Hark! the Herald Angels Sing."*)

Shepherd 4: After the angels stopped singing, the night seemed very, very quiet. My brothers and I looked at each other. We had to go and see for ourselves this thing that the angels had told us about. We had to go to Bethlehem. After all, who could sleep after such a commotion? I was so excited I was sure I would not sleep for days.

Scene Two
(SHEPHERDS *move to stable scene while* CHORUS, CHOIR, *or congregation sings "O Little Town of Bethlehem."*)

Shepherd 5: You might think it would be hard to find a tiny baby in a city. But we had a clue. The baby was sleeping in a manger—an animal feed trough. Not many babies are kept in mangers! All we had to do was look in every stable in the city.

(SHEPHERDS *kneel at the manger. If you are using a light in the manger to represent the baby, turn the light on.* ANGEL CHORUS *or* CHOIR *sings "Infant Holy, Infant Lowly."*)

SHEPHERD 6: When we found him, he was wrapped up snugly in linen clothes, just like the angels said, and was lying in a manger. His mother smiled at us when we told her what had happened on the hillside. She looked as though she had a special secret.

(*For music at this point, choose to have* MARY *or a* FEMALE CHOIR MEMBER *sing "Rock-a-Bye, My Dear Little Boy," or have the* CHORUS *or* CHOIR *sing an appropriate carol such as "Once in Royal David's City" or "There's a Song in the Air."*)

SHEPHERD 7: (*Standing and speaking to audience*) When we left that place that night, we were so excited. We thought it was strange the rest of Bethlehem knew nothing about what had happened. So, we told everyone we saw about the baby Savior. We praised God for the wonderful gift. It would not be long before everyone would know about the tiny baby king. Jesus, the Son of the Most High, had been born in Bethlehem.

(*Have the congregation sing "Joy to the World."*)

THE CHRISTMAS CARD

by Kathy Lindsey

A variety show making use of individual talents

Production Notes

High school students are used in this play to manage the sets. As different groups (Christmas cards) perform, they change props and lighting. Junior high youth who do not sing or play a musical instrument are the announcers. Several can do comical Christmas cards.

To make the Christmas card costumes, take large pieces of posterboard and cut them into Christmas shapes such as a Christmas tree, a candle, a wreath, an ornament, a present, a star, a candy cane, and so forth. Use a simple coloring book for the pattern ideas. Use garland and glitter to add color. You might want to have the parents make the props at home so that the children can practice their song at home. They can also take their props home after the program. Cut an opening for the child's face.

Use a large Christmas tree. Set up the lights so that when you plug in one group of lights, the tree is all red, another group and the tree is all green, and so on with clear, blue, and so forth. This is an easy way to change Christmas card pictures.)

Characters

Announcer
Speakers
Children

9

ANNOUNCER: Christmas cards are a big industry. Most people send them and display the ones they receive. Some people keep them for years. Tonight we are going to present ourselves to you as different kinds of Christmas cards. The nursery children are the first of our singing Christmas cards.

(The younger children enter. Give them their Christmas card costumes. They can sing "Away in a Manger." If your group is too young to sing, they could be a rhythm Christmas card.)

ANNOUNCER: Now we will be entertained by talking Christmas cards.

(Have first through fifth graders enter. They can recite or read Christmas card verses. Some suggestions follow: check your personal Christmas cards if you need more speaking parts. The children can go up on stage in small groups and dressed in different outfits.)

SPEAKER 1: The angels came to tell us of our dear Savior's birth and that he would bring great joy to all and love and peace on earth.

SPEAKER 2: It is time for carols, shopping sprees, hanging wreaths, twinkling lights, trimming trees, Christmas cookies and candy canes, hearts filled with joy, sleigh rides, snowball fights, ringing bells, smells of Christmas, homes full of happiness, laughter, and memories, and snowflakes dancing.

10

SPEAKER 3: May your Christmas be joyful, peaceful, and bright and filled with the love of that first holy night.

SPEAKER 4: Behold, I bring you good tidings of great joy, which should be shared with all people.

SPEAKER 5: Christmas is a time of loving thoughts and heartwarming memories, a very special time to keep in touch with family, neighbors, and friends.

SPEAKER 6: Peace and joy—just two of the reasons we get together to celebrate this wonderful season. We stop and think fondly in a special way of those who are close and those far away. You are thought of with love at this time of year with wishes for a holiday filled with good cheer.

SPEAKER 7: They wrapped you in swaddling clothes and laid you upon the hay. They held you in their arms and gazed into your eyes, and in their hearts they knew that you were the Savior of the World.

SPEAKER 8: Wishing you beautiful Christmas memories to warm your heart now and during the coming year.

Speaker 9: May warm special memories of Christmas past sweetly mingle with joyous holiday moments filling your home with happiness and touching your heart with the beautiful spirit of the season.

(*This following speech works well for a group that wants to go up on stage together.*)

Group: (*In unison*) The joyful lights of Christmas, so festive and bright are warming our hearts on this Christmas night! The light from our windows has a warm and friendly glow from our house to yours comes a cheery hello. The light of our lamp post has a radiance. Flames of candles flicker and dance. Our tree lights are cheerful and colorful, too. We all send seasons greetings to you. Starlight shines down on carolers singing. Stained glass sparkles when church bells are ringing. The warmth of the firelights' luminous glow, the glittering moonlight brightens the snow. And the light that began this beautiful feast is the light of our Saviour. His star is in the East.

Speaker 10: Peace on earth, goodwill to all, the bells of Christmas ring.

Speaker 11: The angels' message still echoes around the world. Fear not. Good News. A savior is born.

SPEAKER 12: Wishing you holly, fir and mistletoe, fireside and candle glow. All the joy that Christmas brings and best of all, a heart that sings.

SPEAKER 13: May all your gifts be made of laughter wrapped in joy and given with love.

SPEAKER 14: Glory to God in the highest and on earth peace, good will toward men.

SPEAKER 15: Wishing you presents 'round your tree, happiness in your home, and love in your heart.

SPEAKER 16: God be with you and bless you during this holy season and throughout the new year.

SPEAKER 17: Angels wings. Music rings. Children sing. It's Christmas.

SPEAKER 18: I wish you heaven in your heart, starlight in your soul and angels in your life.

(If you want all ages to participate in this section, here are some simple pieces for young children. You can also let the parent come up with the pieces as they know what they are likely to say.)

YOUNG CHILD 1: Merry Christmas.

YOUNG CHILD 2: Happy birthday, Jesus.

YOUNG CHILD 3: Love Jesus with all your heart.

YOUNG CHILD 4: Jesus was born. Jesus was born in a stable.

YOUNG CHILD 5: Mary put Jesus in the manger.

YOUNG CHILD 6: There was no room in the inn.

ANNOUNCER: Now it is time for some more singing Christmas Cards.

(*This can involve all the youth, or a particular group. You might want to have all the youth in white choir robes, with a special light on them that changes colors; or have them dress in coats and hats as if they are carolers. Songs are sung. Props can be added for each number, or the singers can wear different hats.*)

ANNOUNCER: Christmas is a time for special music. These next Christmas cards will demonstrate the musical talents of the youth as they play their musical instruments.

(*The youth can play duets, solos, or play as a group.*)

ANNOUNCER: Now we have a dancing Christmas card.

(Have a student who has taken dance lessons perform for the congregation. Add other performances, depending upon the talents of your group. You might have comical Christmas cards that tell religious jokes. If your church has bell ringers, they could perform. If your group includes an artist, let him or her do the set backgrounds or display his or her work at the program. If you have more time to fill, when the announcers introduce each group or individual, have them give a short history of the song about to be performed.)

GET BACK IN YOUR BOX

by Kathy Lindsey

A variety show making use of individual talents

Production Notes

The setting is a living room with a large tree. The tree can be painted on paper and hung on the wall to save space. The boxes that the kids are in should be by the tree. If that is not possible because of a space problem, you could divide the play into acts and add additional boxes with kids in them for the second act.

Older youth can play the adult parts.

Characters

Announcer

Box Persons 1–5

Children

Adults

Props

Large boxes covered with Christmas wrapping. Lids or the tops of the boxes need to be separate from the boxes, as children will be in the boxes. (If boxes are wrapped in plain, bright-colored papers, they can be used in other plays or programs. The boxes can also be used in a Christmas parade. Cut out holes for the head and arms.)

The children in the boxes need to look like toys, like a doll, Raggedy Ann or Andy, GI Joe, a stuffed animal, a clown, a kite, or a baseball bat. Halloween costumes work well.

ANNOUNCER: Sometimes people are concerned that Santa gets more attention than Jesus at Christmas. Hopefully, this play will help with those concerns. Hope you enjoy this play.

(*Scene opens with family and friends in the living room of a house. Very young children can be involved here as they do not have to have a speaking part. A child with a disability could also participate here.*)

ADULT 1: (*Yelling*): Come on, _____! It's almost time to leave for the Christmas program.

ADULT 2: You guys have to get to the church early. You have to get your costumes and make-up on.

(*Others enter.*)

CHILD 1: Not me I got my angel dress on. See? (*Points to dress.*) All I need is my angel halo.

CHILD 2: (*A boy*) I'm not wearing no makeup. That's for girls.

CHILD 3: Me neither, 'cause I'm a shepherd. I follow the star.

CHILD 4: No you don't. I do. I am the king.

CHILD 5:   I am afraid that I will forget my lines and everybody will laugh.

ADULT 3:   Not everyone will laugh because none of your family will laugh. I can guarantee that. I don't think anyone will laugh. Besides your teacher will remind you what to say.

(You can have as many children and adults with speaking parts here as you need. Other children could be talking about their parts in the play. If you have a child who can sing, he or she could even sing a song as if rehearsing it. If you need speaking parts for parents, grandparents, other family or friends, you can choose from the following or come up with your own.)

ADULT 4:   I am sure you will all do a fine job tonight. I am so happy that I am here to see this fine performance.

ADULT 5:   I am glad I brought my camera. I can take lots of pictures for all your cousins to see.

ADULT 6:   We can put some of the pictures in a scrapbook (*or put on the bulletin board at church, or send them to a particular person*).

ADULT 1:   Everybody, get your coats and hats on. It is time to leave. I will go start the car.

(People get on their coats and hats. Older people should help the younger ones. Everyone exits. If you need to extend the length of the play, children can argue about where they sit in the car. Someone can't find his or her coat. The phone can ring. You can have as many boxes as you need to have everyone a part in your play who wants one.)

(Once everyone has left, one of the boxes starts to move. The top to the box comes off and up pops a child dressed like a toy. The youth stretches and then climbs out of the box and yells to the other boxes.)

BOX 1 PERSON: Wake up, everybody, and shake yourselves out of your boxes.

(If this character can sing and dance, have him or her sing, "Shake, shake, shake, shake your boxes." All the boxes begin to shake and wobble and then the lids come off. Characters in the boxes stand up and stretch and/or rub their eyes and look around.)

BOX 2 PERSON: What's going on?

BOX 3 PERSON: Is it Christmas already?

BOX 4 PERSON: What's all the excitement? Is there a fire?

BOX 1 PERSON: Christmas is a week away and there is no fire. I just want to talk to you guys while the coast is clear.

Box 5 Person: (*In a loud voice and using hands while talking.*) I was enjoying the peace and quiet since those loud mouths are gone and YOU had to spoil it all with "Wake up, everybody!"

Box 2 Person: We're awake. Now, what do you want from us?

Box 3 Person: Yeah, we're awake. What do you want from us?

(BOX 5 PERSON *climbs out of his or her box.*)

Box 5 Person: I am not interested in listening to you. I am going back to sleep while I can. They will be home soon and the noise will get bad again. Besides Christmas is in one week. Then all those children will be touching me, fighting over me, and throwing me. By summer they will be leaving me outside for the dog to chew on. Good night!

Box 1 Person: Wait a minute. Didn't you listen to that show on TV last night?

Box 2 Person: What show? or What show are you talking about?

Box 3 Person: The Christmas story about the birth of Jesus. You know the reason for Christmas.

(BOX 5 PERSON *pops up out of box.*)

Box 5 Person: Santa is the reason for the season.

Box 1 Person: No, Jesus is the reason.

(BOX 5 PERSON *points to all the presents.*)

Box 5 Person: Then why all these presents? It's Santa, Santa, S-A-N-T-A.

Box 3 Person: (*Spells*) J-E-S-U-S

(BOX 1 PERSON *sits down in "Thinker" position. Everyone is staring at him. He slowly begins to smile as if he has thought of the answer.*)

Box 1 Person: You know Santa has many helpers.

Everyone: Yeah

(*All the* BOX PEOPLE *come over and sit or stand by the* BOX 1 PERSON *and look at the* BOX 1 PERSON.)

Box 1 Person: Well, (*Pause.*) Santa is one of Jesus's helpers. Everybody knows that Jesus wants his children to be happy.

Box 2 Person: I don't think Santa even knows Jesus.

Box 1 Person: Yes, he does. Just look at this. (*Points to an ornament on the tree.*) It is Santa kneeling at the manger and Baby Jesus is in that manger.

Box 5 Person: If you know so much, why does Santa wear that funny red suit?

Box 3 Person: I know. I know. The red suit covers the wings.

Box 5 Person: Sure. Sure. (*Not believing but playing along*) Why is the suit red?

Box 4 Person: Red is for Jesus's blood that he shed on the cross for our sins. Red should always remind us of what Jesus gave to us.

(BOX 5 PERSON *gets out of the box and joins the others.*)

Box 5 Person: OK, but why does Santa have a beard?

Box 2 Person: 'Cause everybody knows they didn't have no razors in BIBLE times. Everybody had a beard then.

Box 1 Person: You guys are missing the point. Santa represents giving and getting and so does Jesus. Jesus gives love and forgiveness. People get love and forgiveness.

(Offstage noises occur that indicate that the family is back home from the program.)

BOX 1 PERSON: Get back in your box quickly. They are home.

(The older people in the boxes must help the smaller ones back into the boxes. The play can end there, or the family can come in and take off their coats. Someone from the group can lead in a prayer; or the family can form a circle, and each person can say a line. This way some of the children can mention Santa in the prayer.)

THE JAZZY, SNAZZY SHEPHERD BOY

by Shirley Lockhart Ingram

Props

a flute, a star, a Bible

Characters

Narrator
Ethan (a young shepherd)
Amos (a shepherd)
Reuben (a shepherd)
Daniel (a shepherd)
Choir
Angel
Mary
Joseph
Other children

(CHOIR *enters singing "While Shepherds Watched Their Flocks by Night," or they can be seated at one side of the chancel.*)

NARRATOR: Once upon a time many, many years ago in Palestine, often referred to as the Holy Land, shepherds tended their sheep in the lush green pastures and on the hillsides there.

(SHEPHERDS *enter and sit in a semi-circle.*)

REUBEN: Look, men. He's right. There is an unusually bright star.

Twinkle Twinkle Christmas Star

(*The* SHEPHERDS *look shocked, mouths open.*)

(*The* NARRATOR *reads Luke 2:8. An* ANGEL *appears. The* NARRATOR *continues reading Luke 2:9. The* SHEPHERDS *huddle together with frightened looks.*)

NARRATOR: And the angel said to them:

(*The* ANGEL *reads Luke 2:10-12. The* NARRATOR *reads Luke 2:13. Two* CHOIR MEMBERS *put on white sheets and stand on either side of the* ANGEL.)

CHOIR: (*Chanting*) Luke 2:14 — "Glory to God in the highest heaven, and on earth peace among those whom he favors!"

NARRATOR: Luke 2:15— "When the angels had left them and gone into heaven, the shepherds said to one another:

SHEPHERDS: 'Let us go now to Bethlehem and see this thing that has taken place, which the Lord has made known to us.'"

REUBEN: You go ahead. I'll stay here with the sheep.

CHOIR: Baa! Baa!

AMOS: Do you think it's safe to go?

DANIEL: Oh, sure. Come on, let's go.

ETHAN: I want to go too. Please, may I?

REUBEN: Yes, but behave. Be a good boy.

ETHAN: I will. Thank you, thank you.

(*The* SHEPHERDS *exit. The* CHOIR *sings the first three verses of "The First Noel."*)

(*The lights dim while* MARY *and* JOSEPH *enter and sit around the manger.* SHEPHERDS *walk slowly down the aisle and kneel.*)

(*The* NARRATOR *reads Luke 2:16-19.* ETHAN *kisses his flute and gives it to* MARY. CHILDREN *and* SHEPHERDS *Sing "Away in a Manger." On the last verse, the* SHEPHERDS *exit.*)

(*The* NARRATOR *reads Luke 2:20.*)

(*The* CHOIR *sings the first verse of "O Little Town of Bethlehem."*) *In the see the baby Jesus*

NARRATOR: What about the wise men? Don't the Scriptures tell about them? Oh, yes, here we are:

(*As the* Narrator *reads Matthew 2:7-9, the* WISE MEN *walk slowly down the aisle.*)

(*As the* NARRATOR *reads Matthew 2:10-11, the* WISE MEN *kneel at the manger and present their gifts.*)

(*As the* CHOIR *sings* "Silent Night," *the* WISE MEN *leave.*)

(*The* NARRATOR *reads Luke 2:13-15.*)

(MARY *and* JOSEPH *leave, but reenter to center stage.* CHILDREN, SHEPHERDS, WISE MEN, *and* ANGELS *return and stand around* MARY *and* JOSEPH. *All CAST MEMBERS sing the first and third verses of* "Go Tell It on the Mountain.")

(*The* NARRATOR *invites the congregation to stand and sing* "Joy to the World.")

(*The* PASTOR *gives the benediction.*)